Comprehension Crosswords™ Grade 4

Author   Marcia Hemminger
Illustrator   Elizabeth Adams Marks

Table of Contents

EP188R © Highsmith LLC 2003, 2010
4810 Forest Run Road, Madison, WI 53704
www.edupressinc.com
ISBN 13: 978-1-56472-188-4

Go Green

Our environment faces many dangers, such as air and water pollution, global warming, and the loss of natural resources. It may seem like these problems are so big that nothing you could do would help. But, in fact, you can help! Have you ever heard the phrase "go green"? This means changing your lifestyle to help the environment. By "going green," everyone can find ways, no matter how small, to help our planet.

Your home is a great place to start practicing a "green" lifestyle. For example, there are many ways you can save water in your home. Fresh water is a limited resource: only three percent of the water on Earth is fresh water, and only a small amount of that is available for use by people. Saving as much water as possible is very important. By doing simple things, such as taking shorter showers and turning the water off while you brush your teeth, you make a difference. By cutting your shower from 10 minutes to five minutes, you can save 25 gallons of water per day. Another option is to ask your parents to install low-flow shower heads. These actually cut the flow of water in half.

There are also many ways to save energy in your home. Not only does this help save natural resources, it also reduces pollution. The more electricity you use, the more pollution is sent into the air by power plants, which burn huge amounts of oil and coal. You can turn off lights every time you leave a room. At night, make sure appliances such as TVs and computers are turned off. During the day, you can set your computer to "sleep" when it is not being used. This saves the energy it takes to keep the monitor lit for long periods of time. One other great way to save energy is to install energy-efficient fluorescent light bulbs in place of old-fashioned incandescent bulbs. Fluorescent bulbs use four times less energy, yet give off the same amount of light and last much longer. Another great benefit of saving energy is that you will reduce your family's electric bill. You are saving money while saving the planet!

You have probably heard of the "Three Rs": Reduce, Reuse, and Recycle. But how do they apply to you? By reducing the amount of trash you throw away every day, you are saving garbage from going to a landfill. Landfills take up precious space and pollute the air and water around them. What can you do to reduce the amount of trash your family puts out every week? One idea is to reuse items whenever possible. For example, wash and reuse plastic plates and cups instead of throwing them out. When you go to the store, bring reusable cloth bags. Another great way to reduce trash is to recycle. Aluminum cans, plastic bottles, cardboard, paper, glass jars, and many other items can be sent to a recycling center to be made into new products rather than sent to rot in a landfill. Look around your home for all of the things you can recycle.

Once you start to "think green," you'll see opportunities everywhere. Spread the word by talking to your family and classmates about what you are doing. Talk to your teacher about green class projects, such as planting trees or adopting a highway or stream to clean up. You might even brighten up your classroom by planting an indoor garden using plastic take-out containers or old margarine tubs. The possibilities are endless!

Go Green

Across

2. Air _____ comes from cars.

4. Pollution harms our _____.

6. Shorter showers can save 25 _____ of water per day.

8. _____ aluminum cans to reduce trash.

10. By practicing a _____ lifestyle, you can help save the planet.

12. Turning off appliances saves _____.

13. A place where trash is buried

14. _____ is a limited resource that you can help save by taking shorter showers. (two words)

15. By saving energy, you can also save _____.

Down

1. Power plants produce _____.

3. Fresh water and petroleum (two words)

5. Bring _____ cloth bags to the store.

7. Type of lightbulb that uses four times less energy

9. This can be set to go to sleep to save energy.

11. _____, reuse, and recycle.

Marco Polo

Imagine being one of the first people to learn about a distant land and culture. For Marco Polo, his life exploring the East was just that. He traveled across half of the world. He met people and visited places that others had only heard about. On his trips, Marco Polo explored rich cities, saw amazing places, and met interesting people.

How did this experience begin? Marco Polo was born in Venice, Italy, in 1256. Marco's family was made up of rich merchants, or people who made a living by buying and selling goods. Venice is a port city, and his father, Niccolo, and uncle, Maffeo, traveled the Mediterranean Sea to buy silks and spices. Most goods traveled the "Silk Road" and the "Spice Route" that stretched from China to the shores of the Black Sea. Products moved by a series of trades, barters, and purchases by merchants along these routes. In 1260, Marco's father and uncle decided to travel the routes themselves. On their first trip, Niccolo and Maffeo were gone for nine years. They were caught in a war between rival Mongol tribes, where they met the Mongolian emperor, Kublai Khan.

When Niccolo and Maffeo left Asia, they promised Kublai Khan that they would return. In 1271 they made the trip again. This time they took 17-year-old Marco. The difficult journey to China took three years. Marco Polo looked, listened, and asked questions. He watched how people lived, and he tasted new foods. The party finally reached Mongolia to meet emperor Khan, who celebrated their return with a great feast. According to Marco Polo, Kublai Khan was the "mightiest man in the world today, in subjects, territory, and treasure." Marco admired the rich cities, fine palaces, beautiful gardens, and inventions, such as paper and porcelain, that were unknown in European lands.

Marco's father and uncle traded goods in China. Marco, however, was sent on long journeys as a messenger (or spy). He visited Tibet, Burma, Benga, and Laos. He met many fascinating people and heard fantastic tales. After 20 years, Marco wanted to go home. He got permission to escort the Mongol princess, Kokachin, and her servants to the Middle East, where she was to marry. The journey took 18 months

and was filled with danger. Only 117 of the original 700 people survived the trip. Marco finally arrived back in Venice in 1295, three years after his journey home began.

In 1298, Venice was at war with Genoa. Marco was captured and thrown into prison. While he was in prison, he met a writer named Rustichello. Marco told of his adventures, and Rustichello wrote them all down. Most of what was written was true, although there were some exaggerations. Marco went back to Venice in 1299. His book became very popular, and it was translated into many languages. No one repeated these travels for almost 500 years.

Marco Polo

Across

2. Marco went with his father and uncle on a long _____.
3. Marco's uncle and father were gone _____ years.
4. Marco was a messenger or _____.
5. Niccolo and Maffeo traveled the sea to buy silks and _____.
6. Marco's journey to _____ took three years.
7. Name of Mongolian emperor (two words)
8. Chinese inventions included _____ and porcelain.
12. He helped write stories about Marco Polo's adventures.
13. The Silk Road is named after these Chinese fabrics.
14. There was a war between rival Mongol _____.
15. City where Marco Polo was born

Down

1. Kublai Khan was a _____ emperor.
3. The name of Marco's father
4. The trade routes stretched from China to the Black _____.
7. Name of a Mongolian princess Marco escorted to the Middle East
8. Marco's family name
9. Venice is a _____ city.
10. A person who buys and sells goods
11. It was 500 _____ before anyone made the same trip Marco made.
13. Marco thought Kublai Khan was "the mightiest man... in _____, territory and treasure."

George Washington Carver

Think of ways you and your family use peanuts—eating peanuts, peanut brittle, peanut butter, cooking with peanut oil... anything else? You might be surprised to learn that George Washington Carver found 300 ways to use peanuts! He discovered how to make ink, soap, shampoo, dye, medicine, glue, candy, and more from peanuts. He became known as the "peanut man."

Who was George Washington Carver? He was born on a farm near Diamond Grove, Missouri, in 1865 as a slave for the Carver family. The Carvers were immigrants from Germany. Though they did not like slavery, they bought an African-American woman named Mary to help with the farm. Mary had two sons, Jim and George. When George was just a baby, he and his mom were stolen. The kidnappers had planned to sell them for the money they would bring. The Carvers found George and brought him back to the farm, but his mother was never seen again.

As he grew up, George was fascinated by nature, especially plants. Farmers did not have time to plant flowers on their land. However, because George loved looking at and drawing flowers, he secretly planted a flower garden near the woods. He began to paint pictures of the beautiful plants as they grew. George wanted to learn more about nature, so the Carvers sent him to school in Diamond Grove. Unfortunately, the school told him that he could not attend. They did not accept African-American students. The Carvers then sent him to a private teacher where George did well and learned everything he could about science. In 1877, George left the Carver farm and attended an all-black school. He graduated and then traveled and worked for the next 10 years. He had many jobs, including a cook and a janitor. He even started a laundry business. Once, he found out that his mail was being delivered to another George Carver. He added the initial "W" to his name. People said that it must stand for Washington, and so he became known as George Washington Carver.

George then applied and was accepted at the Highland College in Kansas. Again, when he arrived, he was turned away because he was black. So he went to Simpson College in Iowa, where he studied art. He changed his focus from art to botany, the study of plants, at his art teacher's suggestion. When he graduated in 1894, he stayed to teach and run the school's farm. He then went to the Tuskegee Institute in Tuskegee, Alabama. There, he was both a student and teacher of botany. He spent most of his life teaching African-American students at the Tuskegee Institute. He also taught farmers how to grow healthy crops and wrote newsletters explaining new and successful ways to grow these crops.

In 1904, he started a school on wheels. He went to farms all over the South, teaching the science of farming. In 1921, he went to Washington, D.C., and talked to Congress about peanuts and the value peanuts had for farmers. He showed the members of Congress over 100 uses for peanuts and wanted Congress to pass laws to protect peanut sales. He won their support. He became known worldwide for all of his achievements and received many awards for his work and inventions. Someone once asked in an interview why he had not patented all of his inventions, and he replied, "God gave them to me, how can I sell them to someone else?"

George Washington Carver

Across

2. George Washington Carver is known as the _____. (two words)

3. George found 300 ways to use these.

5. The study of plants

8. The Carvers were immigrants from _____.

9. George was born on a farm near here. (two words)

15. George taught _____ how to grow healthy crops.

17. George did not want to patent these.

18. George developed a traveling school on _____.

19. George was born a _____, but his owners treated him well.

Down

1. George's family name

4. A product George made from peanuts to clean hair

6. George's mother's name

7. George showed _____ the uses of peanuts in order to get laws passed.

8. _____ Washington Carver

10. George attended this institute.

11. George and his mother Mary were _____, and Mary was never seen again.

12. George was fascinated by _____.

13. George planted these secretly.

14. George wrote newsletters on how to grow these successfully.

16. George was accepted at _____ College in Kansas.

Orcas

You have probably heard of orcas, or killer whales. You may have seen them in movies or at an aquarium. But did you know that orcas are closely related to dolphins? They are actually the largest member of the dolphin family. An orca can weigh six tons and grow to 32 feet long. This means they are sometimes as large as a school bus!

Because orcas are mammals, they come to the surface to breathe air through a blowhole on the top of the head. Orcas are fierce predators—but not to humans. Orcas are sometimes called killer whales because of their diet—they hunt whales and other marine mammals, such as seals and sea lions. They also eat fish, squid, and birds. They hunt in pods, which are family groups of five to 30 whales. Each pod has its own feeding habits—some hunt marine mammals, while others prefer fish or birds. Pods work together to catch their prey. They often force fish into one area, or they "beach" (slide onto the shore) to scare seals or other animals into the water, where the whales are waiting. On average, orcas eat 500 pounds of food per day!

Orcas are extremely intelligent animals (which is why they often star in shows at aquatic theme parks!). They have unique ways of communicating. In the wild, each pod has its own language. This helps the whales locate each other even when they are separated by large distances. When hunting, orcas use echolocation. This means they send out distinct sounds and wait for the sounds to travel back to them underwater. The sounds bounce back after hitting other animals or objects. The whales can then determine how far away their prey is, as well as its size and shape.

Orcas are easy to recognize, with their black backs and white sides and chest. They also have a white patch above and behind the eyes and a large dorsal fin. The strength of the orca makes it one of the fastest marine mammals—it can travel through the water at speeds of up to 35 miles per hour. The lifespan of an orca can be similar to that of people. Females can live 50 to 80 years, while males typically live 30 to 60 years. This means that on average, a female orca gives birth to five offspring throughout her life. Pregnancy lasts for 17 months. Once the calf is born, the mother is extremely protective of her young. Calves usually stay with their mothers for about two years. At birth, a calf weighs about 400 pounds and measures up to seven feet long. It is born with a light yellow or orange color, which gradually fades to white. When mating, orcas always look for partners outside of their pods.

Orcas can be found in every ocean of the world. The largest populations live in cold water areas such as the Arctic, but they are also spotted in warm waters, such as the Gulf of Mexico and off the coast of Hawaii. They are very social creatures and can often be seen breaching, or breaking through the surface of the water. "Whale-watching" is a popular activity in areas where orcas are commonly spotted.

Orcas

Across

4. Orcas hunt _____ mammals.
6. Length of time a calf stays with its mother (two words)
7. A group of whales that hunts together
9. An orca can weigh up to six _____.
10. To break through the surface of the water
12. _____ are also called killer whales.
13. Orcas can eat 500 _____ of food per day.
14. The type of fin on an orca's back
15. How orcas find prey

Down

1. Each pod communicates with its own _____.
2. An orca can be as large as a _____. (two words)
3. Number of offspring a female has in an average lifetime
5. What orcas use to breathe
8. Orcas are part of the _____ family.
11. An orca has a white _____ behind its eyes.

Secrets to Reading a Map

Have you ever been lost and tried to find out how to get to the right place by using a map? For some people, map reading is as challenging as reading a foreign language. Believe it or not, cartographers, or mapmakers, spend many hours trying to make maps easy to read and use. Learning to read a highway map is a must for travelers on the road. Learning to read a highway map can also help you become a skillful navigator for your parents on road trips.

A map usually includes a compass rose, which shows us geographical directions. Unless otherwise indicated, the top of the map points north. South is directly opposite, or at the bottom of the map. East points toward the right-hand side of the map, and west points toward the left. Knowing this helps you determine which way a road is heading or in which direction the place you are going is located. If you are using a map to find your way while in the car, it helps to turn the map in the direction you are moving. For example, turn the map upside down when traveling south, or rotate the map to the left when traveling east.

All maps have a key. The key is a box that contains information about the symbols used on the map. The symbols may include the lines used to represent different kinds of roads, such as interstates, highways, and toll roads. Often, the color and thickness of the lines identify these roads. The key may contain symbols for cities, capitals, landmarks, points of interest, and campgrounds. There may also be symbols that represent airports, hospitals, restrooms, telephones, and places to swim, horseback ride, hike, and go boating. The key contains a scale, too. This scale shows us how many inches equal a mile or how many centimeters equal a kilometer. This information helps a traveler estimate how far a destination may be and how long it might take to travel that distance. Some keys have symbols that represent the region's physical features, or topography. These symbols show where the mountains, valleys, lakes, and rivers are located. Other keys have symbols that represent political divisions such as city, county, state, and country borders.

Most maps have lines to help us navigate. Maps that show large areas may include latitude and longitude lines. These are imaginary lines on Earth's surface that are used to pinpoint specific locations. The latitude lines run parallel to the equator, and the longitude lines run from the North Pole to the South Pole. Degrees (°) and geographic direction, such as 45°N, mark these lines. Other maps use coordinates that run along the top, bottom, and sides of the map. One side uses letters and the other side uses numbers. These coordinates, listed like "A-3," help you pinpoint the locations of towns and cities on the map.

You can find maps in a variety of places. One of the most common places for a map is in an atlas. An atlas is a collection of maps for states or countries. Individual maps are made for cities, counties, states, countries, or  regions. Small maps can be found on tourist brochures, flyers for businesses, and on invitations to friends' homes. You can spot a map in a subway, train station, airport, zoo, museum, and many other places. Being able to read a map will help you travel anywhere you wish to go.

Secrets to Reading a Map

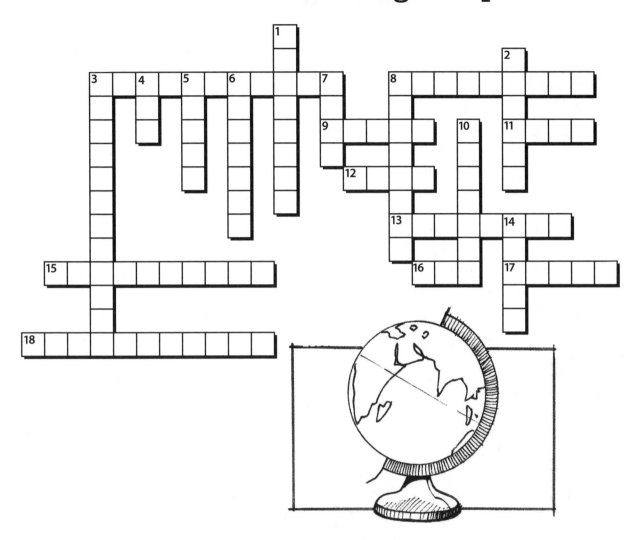

Across

3. This shows all geographic directions. (two words)
8. Lines running north and south
9. The bottom of the map usually points in this direction.
11. It helps to _____ the map in the right direction.
12. A large town
13. The scale of a map helps determine how long it will take to travel a certain _____.
15. A region's physical features
16. A box with map symbols
17. People traveling on highways or _____ should know to read maps.
18. For example, A-3

Down

1. Small maps can be found on a tourist _____.
2. A map of the United _____ might be found in an atlas.
3. A mapmaker is called a _____.
4. What you use to find out how to get where you want to go
5. A collection of maps
6. The key of a map tells what the _____ on the map mean.
7. The geographic direction usually to the right on a map
8. Lines running parallel to the equator
10. You can buy a map for a city, state, or entire _____.
14. The top of a map usually points in this direction.

Glaciers

A glacier is like a river of ice that flows very slowly over land. It is a huge mass of snow and ice that is found in the coldest parts of the world. Glaciers form in places where more snow falls in winter than can melt in the summer. Each year more and more snow accumulates, and at the bottom, the pile of snow is squeezed into ice. Over thousands of years, the ice layer becomes thick and heavy and begins to move.

There are two basic kinds of glaciers. The type is determined by the kind of land and climate conditions in the region. A continental glacier is a large sheet of ice that forms on land and flows toward the sea. Continental glaciers are found in Greenland and Antarctica. The largest is in Iceland. It is three times the size of Rhode Island. As it moves to the sea, it breaks up into huge chunks that crash into the water and form icebergs. The other type of glacier is a valley, or alpine, glacier. These thick "rivers" of ice form in high mountains. They start in small valleys in the mountains and move slowly downhill. The end of this glacier is called a "snout." At the glacier's snout the ice melts into a cold mountain stream. The water is often filled with pieces of rock that have been worn away from the mountains.

Glaciers move, although you usually can't see it. Some move at a rate of a few inches or centimeters a day while others move as much as a yard or a meter. The weight of a glacier causes it to move outward in all directions. Most glaciers move in a downward motion because gravity is the force that makes them move. In 1936 and 1937, the Black Rapids Glacier in Alaska moved more than 100 feet (30 meters) per day. This is the fastest advance ever recorded in history for any glacier in the world. Most scientists believed the rapid movement was due to the very heavy snowfalls that had occurred during the years before.

Glaciers shape the land in two ways. The first way is through the process of erosion. As a glacier moves, it carries tons of land with it. This erosion creates the shapes of mountains and forms valleys and rivers. Often, two or more valley glaciers move down a mountain at the same time. They grind away the rock structure between them. This action produces a pyramid-shaped peak called a horn. One of the most well known examples of a horn is the Matterhorn, which is located in the Alps between Switzerland and Italy. The second way a glacier shapes the land is by depositing sediment, the solid material picked up through the erosion process. When the glacier stops moving, it deposits its load of sediment, most often on the flat land at the foot of the mountains. The sediment deposits can form high ridges and hills. Glaciers have produced some of the most beautiful landscapes in the world.

Scientists who study glaciers are called glaciologists. They measure how thick glaciers are and how fast they move. It is important to study glaciers, for they tell us about the weather in the past and the story of the earth. Glaciologists take samples from deep inside a glacier to get this information. Scientists have also learned how to use the energy of the water flowing from a glacier to make electricity. This knowledge gives us a valuable tool in creating power sources from nature.

Glaciers

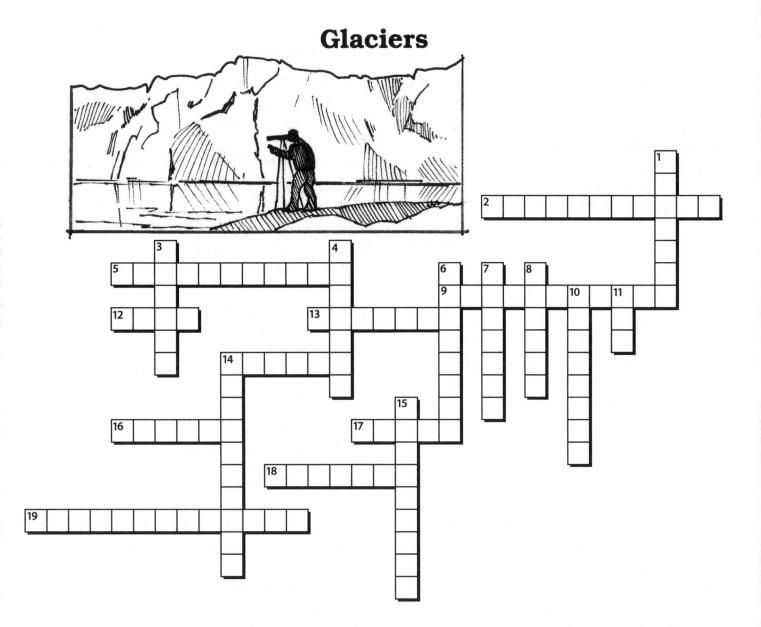

Across

2. The glacier in Iceland is three times the size of _____. (two words)
5. A glacier that looks like a large sheet
9. Flowing water can make this power
12. A pyramid-shaped peak
13. The largest continental glacier is in _____.
14. _____ glaciers form in high mountains.
16. The Black Rapids Glacier is here.
17. The end of a glacier
18. The natural process of wearing away rock or soil
19. Scientists who study glaciers

Down

1. The force that makes glaciers move
3. Electricity can be made from the _____ of a glacier's flowing water.
4. A mass of moving ice
6. A glacier can shape land by depositing _____ when it stops moving.
7. Glaciologists _____ how thick glaciers are.
8. Ice melts into a cold mountain _____.
10. Glaciers break into huge chunks called _____.
11. Frozen water
14. Continental glaciers are found in Greenland and _____.
15. Landforms higher than hills

Jane Goodall

Dr. Jane Goodall is a famous scientist. She is known for her work with chimpanzees and for her unique way of studying wildlife. She was the first person to study chimpanzees in their natural habitat. She is known all over the world for her contributions to the study of animal behavior, called ethology. Her findings have provided us with important discoveries. They have helped not only students of primate behavior, but also naturalists, medical scientists, and anthropologists, who study the origins of humans.

Jane was born in London, England, on April 3, 1934. From the time that she was very small, Jane showed an unusual interest in animals. At 18 months, Jane took a handful of worms to bed to see how they walked without any legs. It was only when her mother explained, "Jane, if you leave them here they'll be dead soon, because they need the earth," that Jane ran and put them outside. When she was nearly five, she disappeared and could not be found for five hours. When she came back, she said she had been in the chicken coop waiting to see how an egg came out. She also began her pattern of observing animals and taking notes at an early age. She had a wide variety of pets in her home. Jane would watch how they behaved and write notes on everything she noticed. This habit became the basis of her method for studying chimpanzees in the wild.

Jane attended secretarial school, but it was always in her mind and heart to go to Africa. "Mum said secretaries could get jobs anywhere in the world, and I still knew my destiny lay in Africa," she told people years later. When she was in her twenties, a high school friend invited Jane to visit her family in Kenya, Africa. She stayed for three weeks and then moved to Nairobi. There, she met Dr. Louis S. B. Leakey, a noted anthropologist and paleontologist (someone who studies fossils). Jane became his assistant secretary. It was with him that her study of chimpanzees began.

Jane was 26 years old when she first went to the Gombe Stream Game Reserve on Lake Tanganyika in Tanzania. British officials did not feel that it was safe for a young woman to go into the wilds of Africa to study animals alone, so Jane took her mother along. She spent many months and then many years watching the chimps and making several important discoveries. She learned that chimpanzees will kill and eat small mammals. Before this, it was thought that they were herbivores. She also saw the chimps making and adapting stems and vines to "fish" termites from their hills. Until then, people thought humans were the only tool-making animals. Jane made visits to the Gombe reserve between 1960 and 1997. During these years, Jane traveled back and forth to England. Here, she wrote books about her adventures, raised money for research, and finished her education. In 1965, Jane received her doctorate in ethology.

Jane is still helping others learn about chimpanzees. She speaks for the World Wildlife Fund and gives lectures to save the earth's primates. She teaches us how to protect their habitats. She warns us of the danger that poachers pose when they illegally kill and kidnap chimps. She has received awards from the National Geographic Society for her work.

Jane Goodall

Across

2. The study of animal behavior
4. People who kill animals illegally
7. Jane was born in London, _____.
8. A person who studies human origins
10. Jane put _____ in her bed when she was 18 months old.
12. Jane observed _____ for many years.
16. Jane was _____ years old when she went to Africa. (two words)
17. She has received awards from the National _____ Society.
19. Jane discovered that chimps make _____ out of stems and vines.

Down

1. Jane studies animal _____.
3. She met Dr. _____ in Nairobi.
4. The group of animals that includes man, apes, and monkeys
5. She worked as an assistant _____ for Dr. Leakey.
6. Paleontology is the study of _____.
9. Jane worked on the _____ Stream Game Reserve.
11. A person who studies science
13. Jane moved to _____ in Africa after staying in Kenya.
14. A friend invited Jane to visit in _____.
15. Jane's last name
18. Jane sat in a chicken _____ for five hours when she was a child.

Insectivorous Plants

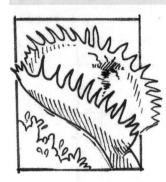

An ant is slowly creeping up the stem of a plant. It is attracted to the sweet smell of the plant's leaves. It begins to crawl across the leaf when suddenly the two halves of the leaf close around it! The leaf has two rows of "teeth" that clamp together, trapping the ant. Soon the ant is dead, and in a few days there is nothing left of the ant but its hard body pieces.

Most plants that we know must take in water and minerals to grow. Nitrogen, along with carbon dioxide from the air and energy from the sun, makes the needed food for plants. That is why most plants grow where the soil is rich in nitrogen. But insectivorous, or carnivorous, plants grow in wet, low-lying swamps, or bogs. Here the soil is acidic and poor in nitrogen content. These plants gain some of their nutrition from the insects they capture.

How do these extraordinary plants work? First, they must have something that lures, or attracts, the insects. These plants cannot reach out and grab or hunt for food. They wait until an insect comes to them. Some plants have a sweet smell like that of nectar. These plants attract flies, bees, and ants. Others give off the smell of decay that lures flies and other insects. There are plants that entice insects with their beautiful, bright colors or leaves with intricate designs. Insectivorous plants are some of the most beautiful plants in the world.

Hidden within these plants are deadly traps that make them very effective at capturing prey. Generally, insectivorous plants have two types of traps: active (moving) traps and passive (still) traps. The most famous plant with an active trap is the Venus flytrap. This white-flowered plant usually contains a half dozen traps that may be as large as three inches across. The traps are leaves that are divided into two lobes that look like partially open clamshells. Spines line the edges of the lobes, and three trigger hairs are arranged in a triangular pattern inside the trap. An insect has to trip two of the three hairs to spring the leaf closed and trap itself inside. The plant then floods the trap with fluids to help it digest the nutrients from its prey.

The other kind of trap doesn't take as much energy. Sundews are a good example of plants with passive traps. There are more than 100 different species of sundews. They grow in swampy areas around the world. These plants produce a sweet bead of nectar that rests on top of tentacles, which are thin, reddish, hair-like stalks that rise up from the plant's flat leaves. The color and sparkling light, as well as the attractive scent, draw insects to it. But once the insects land—watch out! Once, a scientist watched as a cloud of migrating 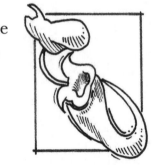 butterflies swarmed onto a meadow to rest before they continued their journey. They never left. The butterflies stuck to the jeweled droplets and could not escape.

Insectivorous plants have suffered because of people's fascination with them. Their bright colors have made them an attractive part of floral arrangements, and they are also picked just for the novelty of having them. They are in danger because we drain more and more marshland and the plants have fewer places to grow. Many of these species are becoming increasingly rare. We must be careful to ensure that these plants continue to survive.

Insectivorous Plants

Across

1. Insectivorous plants live in bogs, or low-lying _____.
3. Venus flytraps trap their _____.
5. An insectivorous plant attracts or _____ its prey.
7. The leaves of the Venus flytrap have three _____ hairs.
8. Most insectivorous plants have ____ colors.
9. Insectivorous plants gain _____ from insects.
11. Fluids help the plant _____ the insect.
15. Most plants grow in soil rich in _____.
17. The lobes of the Venus flytrap look like _____.
19. A Venus flytrap will trap an _____ before it eats it.

Down

2. Some plants attract insects with a sweet _____.
4. A sweet liquid secreted by flowers
6. A well-known active trap plant (two words)
7. Insectivorous plants _____ insects.
10. This type of plant depends on insects for food.
12. Most plants need water and _____ to grow.
13. An example of insectivorous plants with passive traps
14. Some leaves have _____ designs.
16. Butterflies stopped to _____ in a meadow, but never left.
18. A small crawling insect that often gets caught in insectivorous plants.

The Wright Stuff

In the early 1900s, two brothers from Dayton, Ohio, had a dream. They wanted to build a flying machine. Several inventors had already created aircrafts that could fly. However, these crafts were more like kites, with wings that were fixed, or locked in place, and could not be controlled. It was Wilbur and Orville Wright, two self-taught engineers, who finally succeeded at building an aircraft that could be controlled. Their aircraft would become the basis for the modern airplanes we know today.

Wilbur Wright was born April 16, 1867. His younger brother Orville was born August 19, 1871. The boys had five other siblings. When they were young, Wilbur and Orville received a flying toy from their father made of paper and rubber bands. It was this toy that sparked their interest in flight and in learning how mechanical things worked.

The boys seemed to have a gift for inventing. They started their first business, a printing shop, after they built a printing press out of old buggy parts. The bicycle craze of the late 1800s led them to their next venture. After they found themselves fixing their friends' bicycles, the brothers opened a bicycle repair shop in Dayton. They even began making their own bicycles, which they called Van Cleves and St. Clairs. But their interest in flight soon led them to begin plans for their flying machine in the workroom behind their bike shop.

The brothers' first flying machine was a kite made of wood, cloth, and wire. This was useful for trials. They then studied what other inventors had done in the past. Wilbur wrote to the Smithsonian Institute, requesting information about past experiments in flight. The brothers looked at what worked and what didn't. After building their own wind tunnel, they set about testing and building different parts of their machine. They designed the first airplane propellers, as well as the first lightweight engine powered by gas. They were also the first to discover the ideal shape for the wings. But the biggest improvement that the brothers made to their flying machine was to make the wings movable. They found that by adjusting the wings, they could control the direction that the aircraft moved. These improvements set them apart from other inventors.

The Wright brothers built a 600-pound aircraft made of wood and muslin. It had a 40-foot wingspan. After researching rural areas with high winds, the brothers decided to test their invention in Kitty Hawk, North Carolina. On December 17, 1903, Orville took the aircraft on its first shaky flight across the sand. Although the flight only lasted 12 seconds and the craft only flew 120 feet, it was 12 seconds that would change history. After three more flights that day, the brothers claimed an 852-foot flight record.

The brothers would continue to improve their invention. In 1908, Orville made the first flight lasting more than one hour, and the Wrights' planes became the world's first military aircraft. Later that year, Wilbur broke the world record with a flight of two hours and 19 minutes. The Wright brothers were determined to succeed and didn't give up until they did. This attitude paid off. Their invention changed the way people experience the world, and they will forever be known as the fathers of flight.

The Wright Stuff

Across

4. The Wright brothers' first business (two words)
6. They built their own _____ to test their flying machine. (two words)
7. Orville and Wilbur were self-taught _____.
8. The number of siblings the brothers had
10. The weather had to be _____ to test their invention.
11. Their first flying machine was made of cloth, wire, and _____.
13. The aircraft had a 40-foot _____.
14. The brothers made the wings _____.
15. What the brothers repaired

Down

1. Place where the Wright Brothers tested their invention (two words)
2. Number of flights the aircraft took after the first 12-second flight
3. Adjusting the wings helped to control _____.
5. A _____ from their father got the brothers interested in flying.
9. They designed the first airplane _____.
12. The bike shop was located in _____.

Keeping Fit

Keeping fit is an important part of staying healthy and being able to do the things you like to do. It helps you in both work and play. Recent studies show that many children and adults do not get the exercise they need. We have cars to get us places and television, video games, and computers to entertain us. These things make us the most sedentary, or inactive, culture in the world. Now, more than ever, we need to focus on keeping fit.

What are the benefits of keeping fit? It keeps your heart healthy. Your heart is a muscle that grows strong with regular exercise. The heart of a fit person pumps more blood with less work than the heart of a less fit person. Keeping the heart strong through regular exercise also helps prevent heart disease. In addition, being fit also helps people have healthy lungs. Blood picks up oxygen in the lungs and carries it to the muscles. With regular exercise, oxygen gets from the lungs to the muscles more efficiently. Finally, being fit helps keep the muscles strong so they can move freely and easily. You can work and play for a long time without getting tired when your muscles are fit.

To keep fit, you need to do activities that work your heart, lungs, and muscles. Cardiovascular exercises help you strengthen your heart and lungs. They increase your heart rate and make you breathe faster for a longer period of time. Playing basketball, running, riding your bike, skiing, playing soccer, and swimming are all ways to help your heart and lungs stay healthy. To build cardiovascular fitness, you need to do a variety of exercises and be active often. Three ways to build muscle fitness are flexibility, strength, and endurance exercises. Flexibility is the ability to bend and twist easily. A flexible person is less likely to injure muscles because he or she works to stretch and move the muscles often. Being flexible allows you to reach, crouch, turn, tilt, and stretch comfortably. Activities that build flexibility include gymnastics, yoga, and ballet.

Muscle strength is how much force a muscle can produce. Being able to lift, push, pull, or carry heavy objects demonstrates muscle strength. Participating in gymnastics and weightlifting, as well as doing sit-ups or push-ups, all develop muscle strength. Finally, muscle endurance is the ability to continue a motion or action for a long time. Endurance helps a runner finish a long race or a tennis player deliver strong and fast serves throughout a match. Endurance helps you sit still quietly in class for long periods of time or walk to a destination far away. To build endurance, you must gradually play or exercise for longer and longer periods of time. Swimming, hiking, running, and rowing are excellent ways to build endurance.

It is important for you to begin a lifestyle that includes exercise and active sports right now. Studies show that fit children become fit adults. Keeping fit will help you as you grow and develop. Strong muscles will help you have better posture and be able to play longer than children who don't exercise. Now, let's go exercise!

Keeping Fit

Across

1. Skiing, playing _____, and swimming are great cardiovascular activities.
4. Organs used for breathing
5. A strong heart helps prevent heart _____.
8. We are the most _____, or inactive, culture in the world.
10. You can do something for a longer period of time if you have this.
11. Being fit keeps you _____.
12. Exercise in order to keep _____.
13. You have to _____ endurance gradually by exercising for longer periods.
14. _____ is an activity that builds flexibility.
15. Sit-ups and _____ build strength.

Down

2. Having to do with the heart and lungs
3. If you can bend and twist easily, you are _____.
6. Fitness helps you work and _____ longer.
7. You should exercise on a _____ schedule.
8. Muscle _____ is how much force a muscle produces.
9. _____ is a good activity to build endurance.
11. The _____ of a fit person pumps more blood with less work.

Grandma Moses

Grandma Moses was a primitive painter, which means that she never had lessons or formal art training. She was born Anna Mary Robertson in New York in 1860. She grew up on a farm with nine brothers and sisters and had to work hard most of her life. Whenever she had a free moment, Anna would draw. Her father loved to paint, and he often bought long sheets of paper for his children to draw on. Anna Mary used grape juice, crushed berries, and anything else she could find to make her paintings bright and cheerful. She loved bright colors. She once said, "There's no getting away from it, certain colors fascinate me."

In 1887, Anna Mary married Thomas Moses and they moved to a farm in Virginia. Anna Mary had 10 children, although only five lived to grow up. She continued to work hard and started businesses to help earn money for the family. She made "Yankee butter" (a mixture of molasses and bacon fat) and later began selling potato chips. After 20 years in Virginia, the family rented a railroad car and filled it with their household goods. These included chickens, a cow, bushels of apples, a butchered hog, and their dog, Brownie. They moved back to New York, near Anna Mary's childhood home.

It was on their family farm in Eagle Bridge, New York, that Anna Mary began to paint again. At first, the paintings were almost like accidents. Once, when she ran out of wallpaper to cover the fire board that served as a fireplace screen, Anna Mary painted it by hand. She painted a scene with a lake and large trees—her first painting. Another time she painted a window that Thomas saved from an old caboose, covering both sides with pictures. At first she made paintings to give away and didn't take them very seriously. Then, one day Thomas saw a painting of a little boy in blue standing near a fence and commented that he liked it very much. He wondered who had painted it. When he found out that Anna Mary had done it, he commented on how good it was. After that, she began to paint more and was proud of her work.

Anna Mary was now more than 70 years old, with 11 grandchildren and 31 great-grandchildren. They called her "Grandma Moses." Her daughter Anna described a picture she had seen and liked, made of brightly colored yarn embroidered on cloth. Anna thought that her mother could make one that was even prettier, so Grandma Moses decided to try. It was a great success, and she continued to embroider pictures until her hands became too crippled with rheumatism and she turned back to painting.

At the local pharmacy, there was an exchange where women could display and sell the things they made. It was here that a man from New York City named Louis J. Caldor saw her paintings in the window. He liked them so much that he bought them all. He had the paintings displayed in an exhibition at the Museum of Modern Art. The pictures were seen by Otto Kallir, an art dealer with the Gallerie Saint Étienne. He liked them and had an exhibit for Grandma Moses called "What a Farmwife Painted." It opened in the fall of 1940 when Grandma Moses was 80. This show launched her career as an artist.

As time went on, Grandma Moses's art became more and more popular. When she turned 100, President Eisenhower proclaimed Grandma Moses Day in New York State. Grandma Moses died in 1961 at the age of 101.

Grandma Moses

Across

2. Anna Mary made _____ butter.
3. She said, "...certain _____ fascinate me."
4. Her nickname was _____ Moses.
7. Otto Kallir showed her pictures at Gallerie _____ Étienne.
9. Her husband's first name
11. She displayed her pictures in a _____ window.
13. She _____ pictures using brightly-colored yarn.
17. Grandma Moses was a _____ painter.
18. Her married name
19. Grandma Moses was known for her _____.

Down

1. Otto Kallir was an art _____.
3. The man who first discovered her work
5. To draft or sketch
6. Grandma Moses was born _____ _____ Robertson. (two words)
8. In time, her hands became _____ with rheumatism.
10. Otto _____ held an exhibit of her paintings in 1940.
12. She lived most of her life on a _____.
14. Grandma Moses's _____ was called "What a Farmwife Painted."
15. The New York farm was located in _____. (two words)
16. Her first painting was done on a _____. (two words)

Types of Poetry

"Hey diddle, diddle, the cat and the fiddle
The cow jumped over the moon.
The little dog laughed to see such sport,
And the dish ran away with the spoon."

Most of us have grown up reading and reciting nursery rhymes like these. Did you know that these simple rhymes are forms of poetry? Poetry comes in all shapes and sizes. Some poems tell stories; others express feelings or imaginary ideas. Still others describe people, places, and things. Some poems teach us a lesson. Historians have discovered that many of the nursery rhymes we know were actually the way common people were able to complain about the government or monarchy without risking prison or death!

When did poetry begin? It is believed to be as old as language itself. Poetry has been found in Egyptian hieroglyphic inscriptions that date from 2600 B.C. What is poetry? The dictionary describes poetry as "any piece of literature written in meter, verse, or ordinary speech or writing that resembles a poem in form, sound or the like." Some tools that poets use to create poems are rhythm, tempo, rhyme, rhyme schemes, and repetition. Rhythm is the pulse of a poem. It is the regular pattern of sound in music and language. The tempo is the rate of speed in which the poem moves. The content and feeling of the poem should determine the tempo. A rhyme occurs when two words end with the same sound. This repetition of sounds creates an orderly and pleasant pattern. The way that rhyming lines are arranged in a poem is called the rhyme scheme. The scheme, or pattern, is usually shown with letters of the alphabet, such as an "aabb" scheme, in which the first two lines rhyme and the second two lines rhyme. And finally, repetition is when the same word or phrase is used to give a poem a musical quality. In the story of "The Little Engine That Could," the engine says, "I think I can, I think I can..." over and over to help him chug up the mountain. This is an example of using repetition to highlight a part of the story.

Poets paint pictures with words. Poetry is often used as a way of expressing deep thoughts or strong emotions using rich and beautiful language. Poetry looks, feels, and sounds different than other writing, and many people say that it is pleasant to hear or recite. Many types of poetry have special names for the types of writing that are used. Narrative poetry includes epics and ballads that tell a story. Lyric poetry can include hymns, lullabies, and folk songs. Some poetry is based on the number of syllables and lines used rather than on the use of rhyme. Some examples of this poetry are French cinquains and Japanese haiku. Free verse is an unrhymed form of poetry. It is for the poet who wants to create his or her own patterns. The lines in free verse can be long or short and made up of words, phrases, or sentences. The poet decides where to break the lines.

Memorizing and reading poetry are some of the nicest things you can do for yourself. Poems fill your mind with wonderful words, pleasant pictures, and challenging thoughts. Poetry can give you comfort, make you laugh, and even help you remember important information.

Types of Poetry

Across

1. Poetry can be pleasant to _____, or repeat aloud.
2. _____ poetry can include hymns.
3. A type of Japanese poem
4. An unrhymed form of poetry (two words)
7. "Hey_____, diddle"
8. The way that rhyming lines are arranged (two words)
10. A person who writes poetry
11. A rhyme scheme is usually shown with letters of the alphabet, such as _____.
13. Rate of speed in which a poem moves
14. Poets paint pictures with _____.
15. The "pulses" of poems
16. A type of French poetry

Down

1. When two words end in the same sound
3. Poetry was found in Egyptian _____ writing.
5. The repeating of words or phrases
6. Haiku is based on the number of _____.
9. Some poems tell _____.
12. The dictionary describes _____ as literature written in meter or verse.

Photography

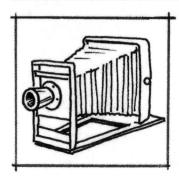

Photographs make newspapers, books, and magazines more colorful and interesting. They record important events. They show us people, places, and objects that we may otherwise not have the chance to see. Photographs help us see other countries and understand other cultures and beliefs. But photography is even more than that; it is an art form.

How did photography start? In 1826, Joseph Nicéphore Niepce took the first photograph. He placed a metal plate inside a camera obscura, or dark box. Sunlight entered a hole in the box and fell upon a sheet of light-sensitive material inside. These first pictures took a long time to develop. The oldest surviving photograph is a view from Joseph's window. The photograph had to be exposed for eight hours.

Jacques Louis Daguerre invented a new device for taking photographs, called a daguerreotype. His images were made on silver-coated copper plates. The plates were made light-sensitive with iodine vapor. When people heard of his new method, they flocked to photography studios to have portraits taken. People often look stiff in these pictures. This is because they had to stay still for about 20 minutes, and it was difficult to look relaxed. Special neck supports were invented to help keep a person's head still while the film was being exposed.

The Crimean War in the 1850s was the first war during which photographers took pictures. For the first time, people could see what war was really like. Taking pictures of war and other historical events was the beginning of photojournalism. Photojournalists are people who take pictures to help report news. As time passed, cameras were invented that made taking pictures faster. Cameras became portable, or easier to move from one place to another. This meant more people could take pictures. Photography took many forms to tell stories, share ideas, and express thoughts. These forms included portraits, landscapes, action shots, and set photography, for which scenes were created.

Up until the 1890s, photography was used as an alternative to drawing and painting. The camera was useful to an artist because it could catch details more quickly and accurately than the eye and hand. In the beginning, photography was considered a shortcut to art. A portrait photographer often took a picture in his studio. The artist then retouched and tinted it to make it look more like a painting. But people began to appreciate the photos as they were. Photographers took pictures that made people gasp in wonder at the expression on a face or the beauty of a landscape, or natural scenery. Individuals began to stand out for their unique styles. Art galleries started to let photographers show their photos in special exhibits. Prizes were awarded for exceptional photographs. Photography was finally accepted as an art form.

Today, photos are everywhere. What photos have made a difference to you? Have you ever looked at a photo and imagined what it would have been like to be there at that instant? Have you seen a photo that inspired a thought or emotion? If so, you are seeing photography as art.

Photography

Across

3. The art of picture-taking
6. Photos of people
8. Short for photograph
9. Jacques Louis Daguerre's invention
10. Joseph Nicéphore _____ took the first photograph.
11. Picture of natural scenery
12. A "dark box" (two words)

Down

1. Person who takes pictures to tell the news
2. Device used for taking pictures
4. _____ entered a hole in the box of a camera obscura.
5. The oldest surviving picture is a view from Joseph Niepce's _____.
7. Daguerre made his plates light-sensitive with _____. (two words)

Bats

Bats are unique creatures—they are the only mammals with the ability to fly. Within the bat family there is an even more unusual animal— the vampire bat.

Not only are they mammals that can fly, but they have another unique characteristic. They are the only mammals in the world that actually feed on blood to stay alive!

These tiny animals are only about two and three-quarters inches long, about as big as a person's thumb. But they can drink up to two tablespoons of blood a day. Luckily, they are not as scary as their name suggests. Vampire bats do not prey on humans. Their blood supply comes from farm animals, such as cows and horses, as well as birds. Unlike vampires in the movies, the bats do not actually suck blood from their prey. They use their grooved tongues to lick it up.

Vampire bats make their homes in caves or the hollows of trees. They even sometimes roost in buildings. They are nocturnal animals, meaning they come awake at night. Vampire bats spend their days sleeping while hanging upside down. At night, they hunt for food.

Believe it or not, vampire bats have something in common with dolphins—they both use echolocation. This is the ability to navigate using reflected sounds. To help find their prey, vampire bats send out sounds with their noses. The sounds bounce off objects such as branches or other animals. The bats can determine how far away something is by the time it takes the sound to bounce back to their sensitive ears. The high-pitched noises cannot be heard by humans. Once the bat has targeted its prey, it does not attack from the air. It lands on the ground near the animal and approaches on all four legs.

It takes a vampire bat about 30 minutes to complete a meal. Vampire bats are so small that sometimes their victims do not even wake up from sleep while the bats are feeding! The prey is not harmed in the process, although the bite can become infected. Vampire bats can also spread rabies, which can be very damaging to cattle herds.

Vampire bats have other amazing adaptations that help them in their quest for food. In their noses they have heat sensors to help them find the area of an animal's body that promises to have the biggest blood flow. They also have special teeth for clipping away an animal's fur, as well as teeth for making a painless cut in the animal's skin. Anticoagulants (anti-thickeners) in the bat's saliva prevent the victim's blood from clotting as the bat eats its meal.

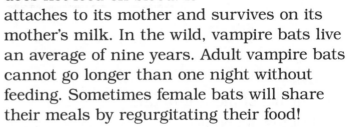

For the first three months of its life, a vampire bat does not feed on blood. It attaches to its mother and survives on its mother's milk. In the wild, vampire bats live an average of nine years. Adult vampire bats cannot go longer than one night without feeding. Sometimes female bats will share their meals by regurgitating their food!

Although fossils of vampire bats have been found in the United States, they now make their homes mainly in Central and South America. While the vampire bat may not be as scary as mythical vampires, all of its unique traits do add up to one pretty amazing creature!

Bats

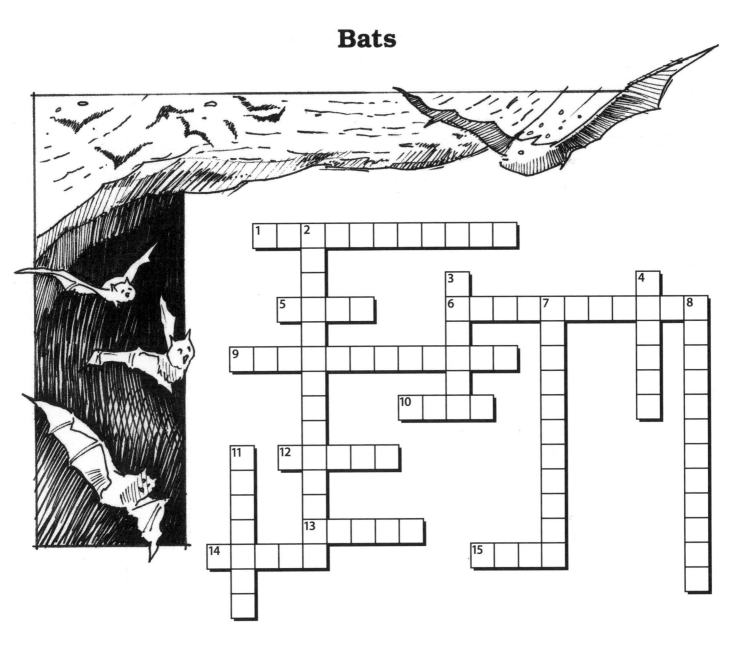

Across

1. Vampire bats use _____ in their noses to locate blood flow on prey. (two words)
5. A baby vampire bat's diet
6. They have many _____ that help them stay alive.
9. Bats and dolphins use this to navigate.
10. They make sounds with this body part to help find prey.
12. An adult vampire bat's diet
13. Vampire bats are about the size of a person's _____.
14. Where vampire bats live
15. The only mammals that can fly

Down

2. Anti-thickeners in the saliva
3. Vampire bat bites can spread this disease
4. Animals vampire bats commonly feed on
7. Vampire bats drink up to two _____ of blood per day.
8. They live in Central America and _____. (two words)
11. Vampire bats are the only _____ that feed on blood.

Answer Key

Page 3

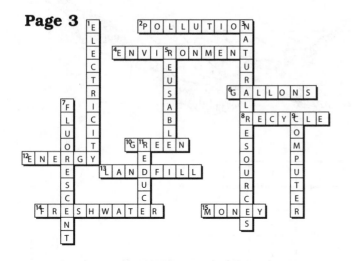

Across:
2. POLLUTION
4. ENVIRONMENT
6. GALLONS
8. RECYCLE
10. GREEN
12. ENERGY
13. LANDFILL
14. FRESHWATER
15. MONEY

Down:
1. ELECTRICITY
3. NATURALRESOURCES
5. REUSABLE
7. FLUORESCENT
9. COMPUTER
11. REDUCE

Page 5

1. MONGOLIAN
2. JOURNEY
3. NINE
4. SPY
5. SPICES
6. CHINA
7. KUBLAIKHAN
8. PAPER
10. MERCHANT
12. RUSTICHELLO
11. YEARS
13. SILKS
14. TRIBES
15. VENICE
KOKACHIN
POLO
SUBJECTS
NICOLO

Page 7

1. CARVER
2. PEANUTMAN
3. PEANUT
4. SHAMPOO
5. BOTANY
6. MARY
7. CONGRESS
8. GERMANY
9. DIAMONDGROVE
10. TUSKEGEE
11. KIDNAPPED
12. CROPS
13. FLOWER
16. HIGHLAND
17. INVENTIONS
15. FARMERS
18. WHEELS
19. SLAVE
NATURE

Page 9

1. LANGUAGE
2. SCHOOLBUS
3. FIVE
4. MARINE
5. BLOWHOLE
6. TWOYEARS
7. POD
8. DOLPHIN
9. TONS
10. BREACH
12. ORCAS
11. PATH
13. POUNDS
14. DORSAL
15. ECHOLOCATION

Page 11

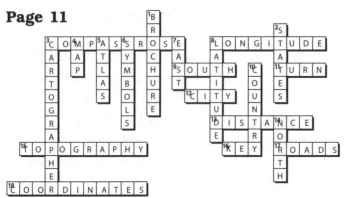

1. BROCHURE
2. SCALE
3. COMPASSROSE
4. MAP
5. ATLAS
6. SYMBOLS
7. EAST
8. LONGITUDE
9. SOUTH
10. COUNTRY
11. TURN
12. CITY
13. DISTANCE
14. NORTH
15. TOPOGRAPHY
16. KEY
17. ROADS
18. COORDINATES
CARTOGRAPHER

Answer Key

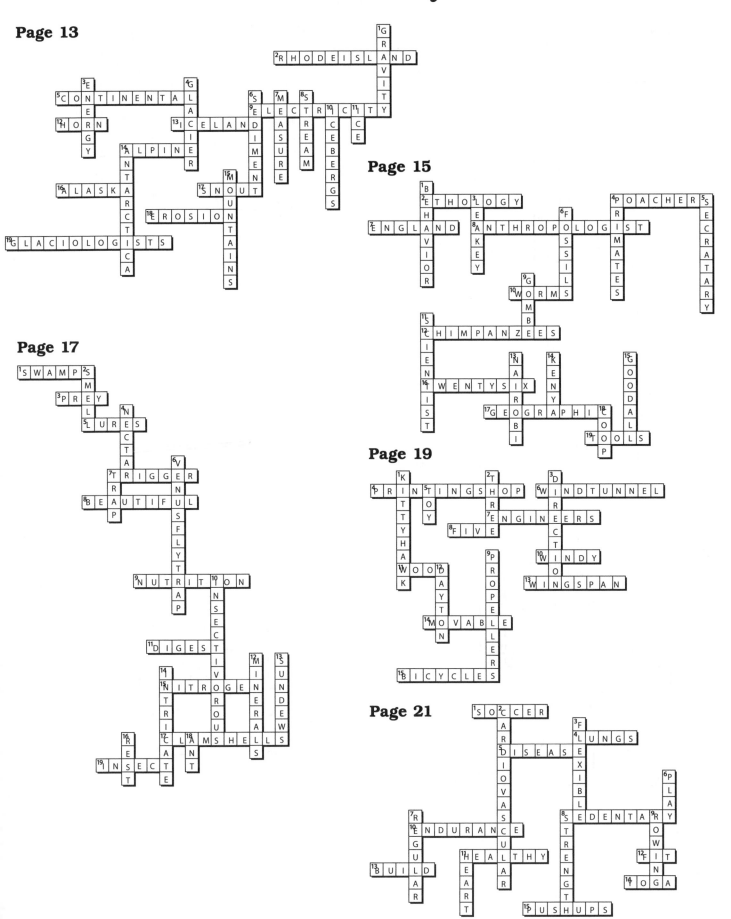

Page 13

Across and down answers shown in grid:

- G R A V I T Y (1 down)
- R H O D E I S L A N D (2 across)
- E N E R G Y (3 down)
- G L A C I E R (4 down)
- C O N T I N E N T A L (5 across)
- S (6 down) M E A S U R E M E N T
- M (7 down) S T R E A M
- S (8 down) I C E B E R G S
- E L E C T R I C I T Y (9 across)
- H O R N (12 across)
- I C E L A N D (13 across)
- A L P I N E (14 across)
- A N T A R C T I C A
- A L A S K A (16 across)
- M O U N T A I N S (15 down)
- S N O U T (17 across)
- E R O S I O N (18 across)
- G L A C I O L O G I S T S (19 across)

Page 15

- B E H A V I O R (1 down)
- E T H O L O G Y (2 across)
- E E K E Y (3 down)
- P O A C H E R S (4 across)
- S E C R E T A R Y (5 down)
- E N G L A N D (7 across)
- A N T H R O P O L O G I S T (8 across)
- F O S S I L S (6 down)
- P R I M A T E S
- G W O M B (9 down)
- W O R M S (10 across)
- S C I E N T I S T (11 down)
- C H I M P A N Z E E S (12 across)
- N A R O B I (13 down)
- K E N Y (14 down)
- G O O D A L L (15 down)
- W E N T Y S I X (14 across)
- G E O G R A P H I C (17 across)
- T O O P (18 down)
- T O O L S (19 across)

Page 17

- S W A M P (1 across)
- S M E L L (2 down)
- P R E Y (3 across)
- N O C T A (4 down)
- L U R E S (5 across)
- V E N (6 down)
- T R I G G E R (7 across)
- B E A U T I F U L (8 across)
- U S E F L Y T R A P
- N U T R I T I O N (9 across)
- I N S E C T I V O R O U S (10 down)
- D I G E S T (11 across)
- M E N E R A (12 down)
- S U N D E W (13 down)
- N I T R O G E N (15 across)
- N U T R I T I (14 down)
- R E E T (16 down)
- C L A M S H E L L S (17 across)
- A N T (18 down)
- I N S E C T E (19 across)

Page 19

- K I T T Y H A W K (1 down)
- T O Y (5 down)
- T R E C T (3 down)
- P R I N T I N G S H O P (4 across)
- W I N D T U N N E L (6 across)
- E N G I N E E R S (7 across)
- F I V E (8 across)
- W I N D Y (10 across)
- W O O D (across)
- D A Y T O N (down)
- P R O P E L L E R S (9 down)
- W I N G S P A N (13 across)
- M O V A B L E (14 across)
- B I C Y C L E S (15 across)

Page 21

- S O C C E R (1 across)
- C A R D I O V A S C U L A R (2 down)
- F L E X I B L E (3 down)
- L U N G S (4 across)
- D I S E A S E (5 across)
- R E G U L A R (7 down)
- S T R E N G T (8 down)
- P L A Y (6 down)
- E N D U R A N C E (10 across)
- S E D E N T A R Y (8 across)
- P O W N
- H E A L T H Y (11 across)
- H E A R T (down)
- F I T (12 across)
- B U I L D (13 across)
- Y O G A (14 across)
- P U S H U P S (15 across)

Answer Key

Page 23

Page 25

Page 27

Page 29